T0210113

Go Find Your Wings

A Journal

AUDREY MAC
INGA AMBROSIA

authorHOUSE®

AuthorHouse™
1663 Liberty Drive
Bloomington, IN 47403
www.authorhouse.com
Phone: 1 (800) 839-8640

Published by AuthorHouse 02/07/2020

ISBN: 978-1-7283-4503-1 (sc)
ISBN: 978-1-7283-4501-7 (hc)
ISBN: 978-1-7283-4502-4 (e)

Library of Congress Control Number: 2020901960

Print information available on the last page.

This book is printed on acid-free paper.

A bird does not fly because it has wings;

it has wings because it flies.

Robert Ardrey

Prologue

Have you lost your wings? There's no time like the present to find them. What a great journey you are about to embark on. It's a journey of self-discovery and revelation. In this book, you will find where you last saw your wings, and when you stopped looking for them. It doesn't take us long to lose our wings, because life unfortunately helps us forget how to fly. That's something we can allow to happen, out of obligation, or fear, or even unconsciousness. When we bring the unconscious to the conscious mind, we can fix anything. Believe it or not, you're very close to finding your way back. The mere fact that you picked up this book puts you in a class all by yourself. You are the one person who can change your reality. It's the one you're living in, and no one is going to come and save you. You must save yourself. There's something you're supposed to be doing, and it's why you were born. Your wings will carry you to your destiny, you just have to find them, attach them, and take flight. See you in the air!

Contents

Chapter 1

Back to the Beginning

"A broken wing simply means, you have to find another way to fly. Have a wonderful day people."

Kerry Katona

When you were born, you were blessed with no knowledge of what life would be like. You didn't know the worries you would have, nor the great joy you would feel. These were the most free years of your life. The title of this book is called, "Go Find Your Wings". When I speak about your wings, I'm talking about the wings that give you sustained lift, high above the ground. The kind that remove all fear of the ground below. The kind that make you forget about the dirt, or the six feet under the dirt. Do you think an eagle worries about what's happening miles below it? Do you think it's counting down its days on Earth, running after timelines and deadlines? The eagle is living in the moment, full of wonder, full of expansive horizon, that goes on forever. Do you know who else thinks like that? Children.

When I think about childhood, I think about unlimited creativity, unlimited happiness, joy, and freedom. A child's biggest worry is what toy they will play with, or which friend is available to play outside in the park. How long they will have to play before they have to come inside, wash up, and get ready for dinner? Children don't wear watches. They dream wide awake, in color, blissfully unaware of the passage of time. This liberating, carefree nature, we tend to lose over time. Let me take you on a brief journey back to childhood.

Answer these questions as honestly as you can:

What were your top 5 favorite things to play with as a child? What did you love about them?

1. _____

_____

2. _____

_____

3. _____

_____

4. _____

_____

5. _____

_____

How did they shape your dreams of the future? Which ones have any relationship to what you're doing now?

_____

_____

Describe in 3 words what it felt like to look back just now.

1. _____

2. _____

3. _____

The reality is, every person doing the exercise will remember childhood differently. Some had an abundance of toys, with difficulty choosing just five. Others can't even remember having five toys. Some remember their childhood fondly, and others are hesitant to stir up the mirky waters they'd rather soon forget. No matter which brush your memories are colored with, the trip back will help you see the totality of the strokes that created the portrait of who you are today. You can't escape who you are, where you come from, nor what shaped your current reality. Retracing those steps can help you change direction. Again, if we remember the eagle, it can see the whole picture. It's the bird's eye view of the map that informs the rest of the way.

If you can balance looking back, suspending the negative emotion attached to it, if there is any, and just looking at the beautiful facts, just as they are, great treasures can be gleaned from the trip. It's easy for me to say that, but it requires courage and practice. We do this all the time, we just aren't aware of it. I'll give you an example.

If you arrive at home from a hard day's work, your spouse asks you, "How was your day?" In order to answer, you have to travel back in time. It's a short distance, but a trek nonetheless. If your coworker asks you, "How was your weekend?", you can bend into yesterday and recount with ease. If your mother asks you, "Remember that friend you had in Kindergarten, the one with the braided ponytails?", you would have to do a backflip through time, but you can come up with at least the first syllable. Do you need to have an emotional attachment to the girl's first name? Not really. Her name is just a beautiful fact. That's all I'm asking you to do here, find the beautiful facts.

Research into the mind, the memories, the past, your own personal history, is a fantastic gift you can give to your present self. Too often, we spend so much time worrying about the future, that we forget where exactly we came from. How can we know where we're going, if we don't look at how we got here? There's a line in a song by Erkykah Badu called, *Didn't Cha Know* that says, "I think I made a wrong turn, back there somewhere." Let's find that somewhere.

Chapter 2

Pivotal Events

*"All you need is the **plan**, the road map, and the courage to press on to your destination."*

Earl Nightingale

Most people are working off the 5-G Life Plan. That plan usually looks like this:

- Grow Up
- Go to school
- Graduate
- Get a job
- Get married

You find out, a little later, that it's not always that simple. There are interruptions in your well-laid plans that come in the form of crisis, financial circumstances, career disappointments, discouraging voices in your environment, and other life stuff that you can pick out of a hat. None of these things are expected, and likely not prepared for. They just show up. So what? It happens to everyone. If you find someone who had a totally smooth ride, most likely the rough stuff is approaching. The rain falls on everyone, eventually. The trick is, what do you do about it. You stop, get your bird's eye view, and regroup.

Let's take another journey, again, we're collecting beautiful facts only:

What were the pivotal moments in your 5-G Plan? When did things take a sharp left turn? Where did the road split?

Growing Up: _____

_____

Going to School: _____

_____

Graduate: _____

_____

Get a Job: _____

Get Married: _____

Describe in 2 words what it felt like to look back just now.

1. _____

2. _____

The best way to illustrate this point is to tell you a quick story. Naturally, the names and likenesses have been altered to protect the innocent.

There was a young woman named, Ilsa. Her mother was a worldly woman, often out with different suitors, not bothering with last names. Well, Ilsa was the product of one of those late nights, and years later, she asked her mother who her father was. Her mother, reluctantly told her, she had no idea, and that she would be better off not asking. This gave Ilsa a sense of not belonging to anyone, including her mother, because she barely saw her while growing up. She was often shifted from relative to relative, until she ultimately ended up in foster care.

A traveling doctor and his wife happened to visit a home to care for a patient, and noticed that the elderly couple caring for the child was not equipped to handle her in their present condition. The doctor and his wife, desperate for children, but unable to conceive, asked the couple if they could adopt the young girl. They agreed. The traveling doctor and his wife, took the young girl, from her present country, Guatemala, and brought her back to the United States. Ilsa, very happy with her new family, often wondered where her mother was, and if she was looking for her.

Over the years, Ilsa went to the best schools, studied with the finest artists, musicians, and professors, and graduated with honors from a prestigious university. She went on to get her Master's Degree in Child Psychology, and a Ph.D. in Cognitive Behavioral Therapy. Her thesis and dissertation analyzed the effects of foster care on a child's development.

In her later years, she spent many days, traveling with her parents to impoverished countries, studying children of foster care. She opened up an orphanage in her home country, and is responsible for the secure adoption of over 600 children. She never found out who her father was, and her mother died years before she ever seriously started looking for her. She adopted a young boy and young girl, and named both of them after her late mother, Ivana. Their names are Ivan and Ivana Marie. She never married, and spends her whole life working for children and supporting her home country.

Can you find 5 left turns in Ilsa's story?

Growing Up: _____

_____

Going to School: _____

_____

Graduate: _____

_____

Get a Job: _____

_____

Get Married: _____

_____

Ilsa's story has a happy ending. Sometimes, left turns aren't always bad. Imagine if Ilsa had no left turns. What if her life continued going the same way, with no deviation? She would not have found her wings. Her wings were clipped pretty early on. Sometimes, your wings look for you.

Your story may be different – you may have lived a pretty happy childhood in a great neighborhood and suffered a setback in high school, college or in your 20's. There are so many decision points during these times that can take you on one road or another. Choosing a career you don't love, having a child with someone you don't like, or making reckless choices that affect your health.

People that blindly run ahead without looking back are clueless of how they got there. Looking back is sometimes, painful. Painful memories carry the GREATEST wisdom. They hold the keys to the greatest jewels of life. Have you ever heard of someone, breaking up with someone, and the next person is identical to the last, just in a different body? How can they not see that? They didn't rise up with their wings to get the bird's eye view. After a breakup, the greatest thing to do is remain alone, take inventory of what happened, and find the left turn. Put down some breadcrumbs, so you know when this same item comes around again, and it will.

Many people just run and grab someone else, because looking back is too painful. Run towards the pain. Run towards the past, clear up that garbage, sift through the rubble and find the jewels, or you will be circling back and be knee deep in it again. Again, return to the scene of the crime to just get the beautiful facts.

Let's take another short journey. Think of the worst relationship you ever had. Think of the person in question. Remember how things were in the beginning. See if you can remember their best qualities, what you liked about them.

Write down those qualities.

_____

_____

_____

_____

_____

Now, write down how these qualities changed:

Write down those qualities.

_____

_____

_____

_____

_____

Here is the tough part. Write down the same qualities this person shared with other people that you've dated before/after.

_____

_____

_____

_____

_____

Guess what? They were like that from Day One. You attracted the exact same person, over and over again. Do you know why though? Because, YOU, hadn't changed.

Why didn't you get the job you wanted?

Why didn't you have kids when you wanted?

Why didn't you keep the house or car you wanted?

Why didn't you get the promotion?

Why didn't you achieve what you wanted?

Why did it all slip through your fingers?

It's all the same answer. You didn't change. You didn't take the bird's eye view of your life, and look at the left turns, put down the breadcrumbs, and recognize when the same "situation" was back to teach you what you missed. Life happens, but we also happen to life. We can affect our lives through our choices, actions, and thinking.

Everyone gets knocked down, that's a fact. What do you do when you're knocked down? Sit there, and expect the tide to turn on its own. No, you get back up, regroup, check the rear view mirror, and collect the beautiful facts, and change direction. There is a cliche that says that men don't like asking for directions, so they will go in circles, driving around lost, out of pride and ego. That is not always the case. Some men don't leave the house without a map, a GPS, alternate printouts, and an extra navigation app to confirm said directions. It has nothing to do with being a man, some women do the same thing, in the same situation, and other seemingly unrelated situations. It is the individual's inability or unwillingness to admit or learn from their own mistakes.

Chapter 3

Personal Limitations

"Limits, like fear, is often an illusion."

Michael Jordan

When did your wings get clipped? When did you first start to notice them loosen and fall to your side? Do you remember the belief you adopted right after? This new truth is called a limitation, or a limiting belief. It's a bump in the road, or pothole that has taken the air out of your personal tires. A flat tire can park you, or get you mobile on foot looking for a solution.

Where do you find that you have limiting beliefs? Check all the apply:

____ **Physical**: I can't do what I'm passionate about.

____ **Emotional**: I don't feel I can go where I need to be.

____ **Financial**: I don't have the means to do what I want.

____ **Situational**: I don't have the freedom because of who I am or who I am responsible for (family, job, location).

____ **Ideological**: I am in conflict with my belief system.

____ **Historical**: I am torn by my past, and it's hindering me.

If you have checked any of the above, try to connect this limiting belief with a pivotal event that birthed it. If you can't see a clear path to your desirable future, what steps have you taken to disprove your limiting beliefs?

Describe 2 steps that you have taken that have failed.

1. _____

_____

_____

_____

_____

2. _____

_____

_____

_____

_____

After your failed attempts, what did you believe about trying again? Which limiting belief was confirmed for you?

_____

_____

_____

_____

_____

Think about one of your goals. Imagine someone that you know that has achieved similarly or exactly what you have yet to achieve. Describe what they did to get where they are.

_____

_____

_____

_____

_____

What do you think they did differently than you? Why did it work for them, and not you? Which factors contributed to their success, luck, fame, money, family heritage, looks etc.

_____

_____

_____

_____

_____

Do you believe they are more deserving than you?

_____

Do you believe there are multiple routes you can take? If so, name them. Be bold in your answers. The wilder, the better. Really get creative.

_____

_____

_____

_____

Describe the best case scenario to achieve your goal. What would it look like if you are standing at the Finish Line. Use emotion words, action words, and describe the scene.

_____

_____

_____

_____

_____

You have just teleported to another reality. You have found some feathers!

Chapter 4

Small Picture Changes

"Change the way you look at things and

the things you look at change."

Fearless Soul Ft Eddie Pinero

Where is the low hanging fruit on the path to fully finding your wings? Remember in Chapter 3, you checked off the personal limitations that were stopping you from achieving your goals. Write them down as though they weren't limitations. For example, if you have a child that is still in school, and that's stopping you from achieving your goal write something like this:

Limiting Belief: Situational

My having a child does NOT limit me from achieving my goal. I am determined to find a way to be a good parent, secure that all my child's needs are met, and still achieve my goal. I will reduce TV time by 30 minutes, and sacrifice 30 minutes of sleep to get it done. I will invest 1 hour a day for a year.

Limiting Belief: Historical

What I have done in my past is not going to determine the ultimate course of my future. I have learned from my mistakes, and I am using the jewels from revisiting my past, to propel me forward. I have forgiven myself from the mistakes of my past, and made peace with them. There is no benefit to holding myself back to punish myself for things I have already grown from. I'm a new person, and I will use the tools of wisdom to create a new paradigm. I will put down breadcrumbs so I don't repeat the mistakes of my past. I will stay conscious and present so my eyes are wide open as I head towards my goal. Nothing will stop me from reaching the finish line.

How EMPOWERING does that sound? You have to talk yourself into a new belief system. The more you believe it, the Universe will rise up to meet you. Think of a horse that doesn't want to be ridden. Nothing on Earth will get that horse to move. If a horse doesn't want to be tied up, you will have to run pretty fast to tame a wild horse. You have to be strong like that. I'm moving forward, no matter what. If there is a barrier, I will jump over it. If there is a wall, I will plow through it. If there is a roadblock, I will take a detour, but this horse is coming through. Period.

Now, it's your turn. Take 2 of your limiting beliefs and rewrite them as empowering statements. It's invigorating to change the story in your own head. You have the pen, and are the only one who has the right to write in the book of your subconscious mind. It may feel odd at first, because your doubt will creep in. Knock it down and push forward.

Limiting Belief: _____

1. _____

_____

_____

_____

_____

_____

_____

_____

_____

_____

<u>Limiting Belief:</u> _____

1. _____

_____

_____

_____

_____

_____

_____

_____

_____

_____

_____

Chapter 5

Realistic Possibilities

*"Take the first step in faith. You don't have to see the whole **staircase**, just take the first step."*

Martin Luther King, Jr.

When you were just a child, you asked for gifts from Santa for Christmas or maybe it was money under your pillow from the tooth fairy. You didn't care how it got there, nor did you care how much it costed. You just knew that somehow, that bike, or dollhouse, or computer was going to make it down that chimney. You didn't even have a chimney, but you knew that Santa was on the job, and he had a sleigh, and he had frequent flier miles, and the how and when was his problem to solve. You knew that if you put that little tooth under the pillow several dollars, hopefully, would magically appear. Let's take that same kind of carefree belief, and turn it into a modern day adult, realistic version for us to chew on.

How would you live your life if you believed anything was possible? What plans would you make if you knew they couldn't fail? How would your mind shift, how expansive would it be, if you had a black card, and no limits? There is a funny saying, "If you have to ask how much it is, it's because you can't afford it." Can you imagine walking into a luxury dealership, picking out a car, and telling the salesman to have it delivered to your mansion? You can't. That's why you don't have it. You are already thinking about how to pay for it, and how much the delivery charge is, and what about the taxes, and what if it breaks down. Can you afford the repairs? The person that says that to the salesman is not thinking about any of that because he or she already knows it's covered.

The stay at home mom is not really trying to get a two-seater that gets up to 200 mph in 60 seconds. That is not realistic for her. She just wants a mini-van with tv screens on the headrest to keep her kids entertained, on the way to the doctor. Her mansion is a 4-bedroom house, with a big yard, and a washer and dryer. Her fantasy is worry-free living. I'm not mad at her either, and there is nothing wrong with not wanting what everyone else wants. You have to find your happy place. I will tell you though, she has just as much fear about walking into that minivan dealership as you have walking into the Ferrari dealership. Her pen is shaking on the dotted line, just like yours would be on that mansion. What's the difference? Whatever you believe is possible.

It's story time. There was a woman who had 7 small children. She moved to a big city from a small country town. Her husband moved to this big city for work, and sent for them when he found somewhere for them to live. The living arrangements weren't ideal, and when she arrived on a 10-hour train ride, kids in tow, his relatives met her at the station. There she was, overloaded with luggage, crowding into a station wagon, with kids sitting on top of the other. When they arrived at the small 2-bedroom house, that her husband's brother shared with his wife, she winced. She thought to herself, "My husband thinks that me and these 7 children are going to sleep in this one room, on the floor? How long is this going to work?"

She found out that her husband would only be there on the weekends, he worked 4 hours away. This was not ideal, but it was what it was. She made the best of it, trying to find work, sewing and cooking for neighbors. She saved every dime she earned. She saved every dime he earned. In one year, she found a house in a neighborhood, that from the looks of the residents, didn't seem like she belonged there at all. There were doctors, lawyers, teachers, and policemen living there. She was a housewife, with a 9th grade education, and no provable work experience. She went down to the bank, got herself a loan, based on her husband's work, found someone to write her a colorful letter, stating that she had all the work experience they were looking for. She doctored up some papers and got into that house with zero money down. Until the day she died, she remained in that house for 50 years.

What was her mindset? "I am getting out of this situation, come hell or high water. Whatever I have to do to change my reality, I will do." This was back in the 60s, and this was a black woman, moving into an all-Italian neighborhood.

She was the first African-American person to move into that neighborhood. She just changed what she believed was realistic and made it happen. She was told no by one banker, and quickly shifted her feet to another one. Guaranteed, she was not going to stop until she heard the words that she already repeated in her mind, "Yes." That woman was my grandmother, and she taught me that nobody can stop a determined mind. The only person that can stop you, is you. Did her circumstances tell her that she could achieve that? No. She blew past that, and shifted herself to another reality. She slapped on those wings, and flew right out of that one room.

In the new house, she had 4 bedrooms, 2 bathrooms, a washer and dryer, a yard for her 7 children, and a place to finally call her own. Was she trying to get a mansion? I believe, if that's what she wanted, that's what she would've had. She kept it practical, and the pebbles appeared across the pond. It's not about what's possible, it's about what you believe is possible. It's not about what's realistically possible, it's about what you believe is realistically possible. As soon as you shift your mind, let the wind catch it, suddenly the different scenarios come into view. If your focus is narrow, that's all you will see.

What do you believe is possible about your goal? How can you level up? What toppings can you add to it to make it deluxe. Think about a scoop of ice cream. What would you do to make it a banana split? Turn your dream into a banana split or a hot fudge sundae.

_____

_____

_____

_____

_____

_____

_____

_____

Write a quick letter to your future self. Tell yourself how crazy you were to believe that this goal was possible. Tell yourself how cool it is that you are at the finish line. Give yourself a high five. Describe how you want the celebration to go. Give them the list of all the toppings you want.

Dear _____,

_____

_____

_____

_____

_____

_____

_____

_____

_____

_____

_____

_____

Chapter 6

Wild Changes

"Yesterday I was clever, so I wanted to change the world. Today I am wise, so I am changing myself."

Rumi

E arlier, we spoke about why things didn't change in your life. We discussed the fact that the reason things didn't change is because you didn't change. There are 3 elements to any human being on this planet. That is the Mind, Body, and Soul. Changes needed to happen on all levels to take effect in this plane of existence.

In my grandmother's scenario, she changed her mind, then she changed her body, got up and did something, and then her reality changed. This made her soul feel rested, because the goal was reached. Accomplishing things makes the soul rejoice, and rebound into a comfortable rest. A soul unrested, is a mind and body out of alignment. Wild Changes propel all circuits into alignment. Remember the old television sets, when they would get out of whack. What did we do? We gave it a good smack. That's what we're going to do right now. Give our mind, body and soul a good smack. A nice smack. One to get the picture clearer.

Think of some wild changes you can make to your mind. Are you someone that tends to be negative? Are you always playing Devil's Advocate when someone has an idea? Are you pessimistic, an optimist, or a spectator? Do you run from conflict, or are you extra confrontational? When you think about your goals, does this help you or hinder you? Describe your own personality in ten words.

1. _____

2. _____

3. _____

4. _____

5. _____

6. _____

7. _____

8. _____

9. _____

10. _____

Don't get freaked out by this next assignment. Now, write down the exact opposite of all these traits.

1. _____

2. _____

3. _____

4. _____

5. _____

6. _____

7. _____

8. _____

9. _____

10. _____

Believe it or not, there are some people that view you this way. Either they are delusional or you are. Either way, somebody is right. Maybe you both are. Some people may be stingy with their husband, but generous with their children. Some people may be polite to the neighbors, but nasty with the people at church. Some people are considered agreeable and a team player, and others see them as a domineering know-it-all. It's all about perception. The reason I had you do both lists, is because we are going to work with them individually.

First list, these are your perceptions about your personality. Next to each trait write a (+) or a (-), meaning they are positive or negative traits. The pluses are things you want to examine to see if they are going to help you towards your goal. If you put for example, that you are an outgoing person that likes to socialize, is that going to help you write a novel? It depends, does it involve interviewing people? If not, then you need to become introverted to get it done. You might need to cut down on your socializing, and hunker down into some alone time.

Another example, if you put down that you are a frugal person, but you want to sell luxury houses, you're going to have to spend some money on some nice threads so you can look the part. You might need to drop some cash on a professionally designed website, business cards, and a marketing team to get it going. Being cheap won't get you where you want to be. Let's say you put down that you are reserved a.k.a. shy, and you consider this a positive trait. If you want to be a public speaker, this won't do. There are some wild changes you need to make to your personality to match your goals.

If you put down that you like the finer things in life, designer brands and such, but you say you want to save up for a house, that's out of alignment with saving money for a down payment. Spend a few minutes thinking carefully about the personality of the person that has what you want to achieve. Rewrite it here.

1. _____

2. _____

3. _____

4. _____

5. _____

6. _____

7. _____

8. _____

9. _____

10. _____

Now, for the second list. This is how you are perceived by others. This will determine who you can enlist to help you reach your goal. Some goals can be reached all on your own, but you may still need someone to buy the product. If people's perception of you is misleading, take a look at how you are projecting yourself. See if you can tweak your presentation to the public.

If you are so bold, gather a group of your friends, and ask them to describe your personality in 10 words. You will be surprised at how random the traits are. You think you are one way with everybody, and that's just not the case. Each person will view your generosity or lack thereof a different way. Some will find your outgoing nature garish and draining, other people can't get enough of you. Pick a nice mix of people, and make sure they don't put their names on it, so there are no repercussions for blatant honesty. Be prepared for the raw truth. You can't change unless you get down to the nitty gritty. Regroup and refine.

On this list, you will look at the opposite characteristics you wrote down on the second list. Write down certain people that you are that way with, and why.

1. _____

2. _____

3. _____

4. _____

5. _____

6. _____

7. _____

8. _____

9. _____

10. _____

Between both lists, design how you would like to see yourself. Keep in mind, any of these traits can hold you back or propel you forward. Think of ways you can change your personality so it matches the person who has achieved your goal. Be willing to gut and strip it all. Go Wild!

Chapter 7

Rebirth/Spawn

"It's never too late to become who you want to be. I hope you live a life that you're proud of, and if you find that you're not, I hope you have the strength to start over."

F. Scott Fitzgerald

N ow that you've gotten your new marching papers on your personality, let's talk about your body. What are you going to DO differently. Personality is in your mind, how you think, how you feel, but how does that translate to your body? You can say that you aren't going to be stingy anymore, but what does that look like in real time? Are you going to be actively more generous, or are you just going to talk about it.

This section is all about action. What are some things that get you motivated? Here are some quick fire questions that should just roll off the top of your head.

What's the song that gets you dancing?

_____

What's the one place, if you're invited, is always a Yes?

_____

Who is the one person that makes you light up when you see them?

_____

If something good happened, who is your first call?

_____

Which food takes you to your happy place?

_____

Which movie could you watch over and over?

_____

What hobby do you have that brings you joy?

_____

What is the scent of your favorite candle?

_____

What is your go-to self-care regimen?

_____

What secret talent do you have that no one knows?

_____

What prominent person would you like to meet?

_____

What figure from history would you bring back to life?

_____

What's your favorite color?

_____

Why is that your favorite color?

_____

What is your spirit animal? Why?

_____

_____

_____

That should have gotten your adrenaline pumping? All we talked about were things you love. Love is the great motivator. If you need to get motivated, go do something you love, and then work on your goal. Use that same energy to power yourself through.

You might want to look at how much you do the things you love. You might want to look at how much your favorite color is actually around you. Is your favorite scent in your bathroom, your job, your car refresher, or body wash? If not, why not. How often do you hang out with your favorite person? How much do you know about the prominent figure you would bring back to life? Bring them back to life by reading everything about them. Is your spirit animal in a picture on your wall?

Do you listen to your favorite song first thing in the morning? Do you treat yourself to your favorite food, or give yourself a nice break with a self-care regimen? You can't work off of fumes if you want to bring this goal to fruition. You have to be operating from a full tank. Nobody is going to fill your tank like you will. Make the energetic force around you as positive as possible, so you remain in a creative space. It's these little things that add up over time. They birth a new version of you, one that is happy, joyful, excited, motivated, and full of energy to make moves.

Imagine getting a call from a friend to run a marathon when you've only had 2 hours of sleep. You would say, "Uh, no I don't have enough in the tank to do that." Your goal is a marathon, not a sprint. It's going to take work, and you are going to have to be rested up for twists and turns that come your way. Disappointments may pop up, but you reach back, and put it into second gear. You can't do that when you're tapped out. You have to fill yourself up with good stuff, so when the hits come, you just keep on rolling. This is intentional, and a conscious effort on your part, to give yourself the best chance to endure until the end.

Here is the fun part. Write down a step you will make towards your goal, every time you enjoy one of your treats above. For example:

Favorite color: Brown Sienna

Task: Write 100 words in my book

Reward: Buy myself something in my favorite color.

Favorite food: Macaroni and cheese

Task: Make 5 phone calls to potential investors

Reward: Make a pan of mac 'n cheese to share.

You can even flip it around and get your reward first, and if you are your own accountability partner, you will be motivated to equalize the system by performing the task the second you get home from buying your new shoes. Whatever works for you. If you try this Motivation Technique, you will get more done, faster than you ever thought possible.

Try it now: Pick 5 things that motivate you to act and assign a task and a reward to match your ultimate goal.

Favorite _____

Task: _____

Reward: _____

Favorite _____

Task: _____

Reward: _____

Favorite _____

Task: _____

Reward: _____

Favorite _____

Task: _____

Reward: _____

Favorite _____

Task: _____

Reward: _____

Favorite _____

Task: _____

Reward: _____

Favorite _____

Task: _____

Reward: _____

Favorite _____

Task: _____

Reward: _____

Favorite _____

Task: _____

Reward: _____

Favorite _____

Task: _____

Reward: _____

Chapter 8

Hail Mary

"The critics are always right. The only way

you shut them up is by winning."

Chuck Noll

Can I still win? You will find an inevitable fork in the road, on the journey to your destination. Very often, the road gets rocky. That's good news, because if you were standing still, you wouldn't be at this point. The roadblocks only effect moving cars. That's when you need to celebrate. You're one step closer. What do you do now?

Now, is a good time to get some reinforcements. There are people in your environment, family, workplace, or neighborhood that need to know what you're doing. It's not to brag or boast, and it's not even to get their approval. It's to put it out into the universe in more than one person's mind that this "thing" is happening. How do you let them know in the most subtle way possible? In casual conversation. It's important to leave this for when things are already moving.

Many people have the tendency to knock an idea down before it gets started. This cancels all that. If you tell them you are knee deep in writing a science fiction novel, they can't talk you out of starting. Keep quiet until the wheels are already moving. Just casually drop in that you are working on something that will be done by the end of the year. Be careful about giving dates, because those can move, and you don't want to put yourself under unnecessary pressure. If you finish early, kudos to you. If you finish later than expected, nobody knows when it was due so you keep that tidbit to yourself.

Here is an example of why this is good to do. Let's say you want to create a wedding decorations company. While you're getting your business documents in order, you can casually let a newly engaged couple know that you are almost up and running, and they can be your first client at a reduced rate. They will love to hear that, because they're about to find out just how expensive that can be. Instead of buying a ton of fabric, ornaments, and centerpieces for a wedding that doesn't exist, your first order can be custom to them. This is thinking smart. Start marketing before you even have something to show. As soon as you get a confirmed yes, and a deposit, start marketing that wedding as though it's already happened.

Tell your friends, neighbors, coworkers, mailman, whoever, that you are working on a wedding in June, and the bride is just tickled pink with your custom creations. You know news travels fast. Let them be your volunteer marketers. They are going to tell your business anyway, so give them something to tell. Before long, the right set of people will hear that you do weddings, and Client #2 has manifested. The roadblock is in the rear view mirror.

If you go to church, put your business in the church announcements. Mention it at choir rehearsal. Ask the pastor when the next wedding will be. Get assertive. Approach them. Tell everybody what you're doing, even the lady in the checkout line at the grocery store. I don't believe in the words, "shameless plug". What is there to be ashamed about? People have no problem blasting their personal business all over social media, oversharing, why can't you overshare your personal goals. You never know who could be watching, just like you never know who is watching your bachelorette party pictures. Put out there what you want to spread. You could actually be motivating others as well.

Think about all the social media platforms you visit regularly. How many of your followers know what you're trying to do? Have you ever shared your goals with them, or are you just there scrolling through other people's goals? Get active, and put your hat in the ring. Again, make sure you have done some good work on it first. People let others talk them out of even starting good ideas. This nips that in the bud. Start, then share.

Please, be aware, the naysayers will come. It's math, they will always be there. It's their job. They are just being used by the Universe to test if you have the chops to keep going. Don't worry about it. I wouldn't even pay them too much mind, unless they live in your house. Keep imagining, a ping pong table, and instead of sending the pong back across in a meaningless conversation of tit for tat, let it roll off the table.

This is easier said than done, but with practice, you won't even feel the need to respond at all. It's beautiful to watch them squirm trying to get a rise out of you, but your head is so far up in the clouds, looking down at the map of your future, wings flapping so loud, you can barely hear them.

Don't feel ashamed of declaring, "I'm a writer, or web designer, or wedding planner, or chef, or musician." Who are they to decide when you can say it? The past, present and future, are always happening in the now. So, claim it and walk boldly into it. Think of 5 places online or in person, that you can let the world know what you're planning to do. Remember, speak about it as though it's already done.

1. _____

2. _____

3. _____

4. _____

5. _____

Can you hear that second wing flapping? It's looking for you, just like you're looking for it. Sometimes, you have to get around people that have what you want. Get around some people that are already flying and well on their way. You have to suspend your tendency to compare their journey to yours in an unfavorable way. It doesn't matter how fast they achieved what you want. There's no time limit on it. I recently saw a 90-year old woman walk across a stage, achieving her first doctorate. Guess what? She still wins. The crowd roared louder for her than anyone. She was in the company of other eagles who had what she wanted.

Find your group of eagles. Either there is an association for what you want to do, a club, an online chat room, or a coffee shop networking event. You can achieve so much more when you share with others going the same route as you. Have you ever shared a cab with someone that you met at the airport. Pay twice for what? Some of them have already transcended what you're going through now, and you can stand on their shoulders.

Don't be too proud to beg for advice. There are those that will get intimidated by the newcomers, fearing that someone is going to take their spot, and those are chickens. I'm talking about eagles, that have no fear that you will take their space in the sky. They come from the school of thought, that the Universe is infinite, and there is more than enough to go around. Use your discernment, and don't share too much with the chickens. They only know what it's like to fly across the fence, and there isn't enough corn on the ground for them. Get around some real winners, bald eagles, that ride the thermal wave and see the world in a plentiful way. They won't mind giving you a hand up, because someone likely did it for them.

Think of 5 places you can go to join your special group of eagles to help you find your wings. Do real research. Be willing to spend some money to join. Invest in yourself.

1. _____

2. _____

3. _____

4. _____

5. _____

Chapter 9

Timelines

"I like to challenge myself and give myself a timeline.

It pushes me to be more creative and actually do

these things, not just dream about them."

Balthazar Getty

There is a difference between timelines and deadlines. The word deadline has the word "dead" in it, which gives the impression, that if it's not done at that time it's dead. We are working on a different principle. Timelines include the word "time", which means the passage of time will bring the goal to fruition as a certainty. One is based on fear, the other is based on faith and belief.

Let's get this down. Get your calendar out, let's set some timelines. You may have a monthly calendar, but if you want to get into the microscopic details of your day-to-day movements, get a weekly calendar. This way you can set goals on a 7-day cycle. The next level would be a daily calendar with To-Do lists. My favorite thing about To-Do lists is that subconsciously, my mind believes that everything on this list must be done today. My whole being just gets into action, not even taking into account that some can be put on tomorrow's list. I make my To-Do lists every day, from scratch. It's a nice time you can have with your internal team, your mind, body and soul. You ask them, "What are we going to get done this day?"

When making To-Do lists, try not to put things on the list that can't be done today. It's the small wins that keep us motivated. For instance, putting an item like, "Write book" is not as effective as, "Write 2 pages". One is very likely to end up as a win, the other is not definitive enough to celebrate. The same item will have to be copied and pasted throughout the rest of the month. It's not exciting. One day you could write, "Write 3 pages", and the next day, "Write 3 paragraphs". Both are equally likely to end up as wins. The more specific you become, the more your mind will spur your body into action. When the task is completed, the soul is happy. The reason I say make your lists daily is because, some days you can't do anything. If you write lists beforehand, you aren't factoring in what's possible that day. You are setting yourself up for failure when you don't check in with your team to see what's on the menu for the day. The weekly goals can be a mixed bag, simply because you can mix and match as you see fit. Monthly goals are more of a check-in to inform the daily and monthly goals.

Don't forget to celebrate your small wins. Get yourself some stickers, or pretty colored markers to highlight the days you get your whole list done. Looking back on that is more motivating than you can imagine. Children like stickers for a reason, it feels awesome to be recognized. It feels even more awesome to recognize yourself for what you achieved for you. Go ahead and get your calendar out, even if you have to print a few. Start off with a quarterly plan, 3 months out.

Take a couple hours and really hash it out. If your goal is something that will take a year, print out a whole year's worth of calendars. Spread it out all over the table so you can see the whole map with a bird's eye view. From start to finish, track your progress. Give yourself percentage markers when you're halfway there. Don't ignore how encouraging these little mile markers can be. They're for your eyes only.

Even if you don't know how you're going to get something done, put it on the monthly calendar anyway. For example, if you need to write a press release, you may have never even seen a press release. Don't worry about that. Put it on the calendar, and sometime before that day, write down the research you will need to find a press release that matches what you need to write. Take a press release writing course online. Contact a friend or a freelancer and bounce some ideas around. By the time that deadline shows up, you would have it already done.

If you want a special job, don't worry about how you're going to get that job. In the months before you are to have that job, fill in your job search time, your resume rewriting time, improving your interview skills, and your wardrobe refresh time. Put it all down on the calendar. Keep it on your refrigerator, or your bathroom wall, or even next to your dinner table. Instead of watching television, read over your goals. Keep it at the front of your mind, and think of nothing else. That will make it appear before your eyes in no time.

Which goal are you going to put on your calendar?

_____

How long will it take to reach this goal?

_____

Will you be using a monthly calendar?

_____

How many months do you need to use?

_____

Will you be using a weekly calendar?

_____

Will you be using a daily calendar?

_____

Will you be making fresh daily To-Do lists?

_____

Which visual reward system will you use when you win?

_____

_____

Chapter 10

Execution Plan

"Innovation is rewarded. Execution is worshipped."

Eric Thomas

What is it going to take to build your last wing? How are you going to attach it to your back? What perch are you going to leap from? When you take flight, how will you sustain the momentum until you get to the mile high status? When you hit those rough atmospheric winds, when turbulence arrives, what's your game plan?

One thing that motivates me is quotes. As you can see every chapter has a quote to introduce you to the topic. These are great to print out and put into a nice frame. Sprinkle them around your home, or job, and regularly look at them to give you that jolt of power. You'll feel your back instantly straighten up when you read the right one. Try to find quotes that really get your engines revved up.

Think of an author or celebrity that you really admire. Write down something they would say. If you want, when you're typing the quotes into your computer, put your name in it. Then, sign it with their name. It's so much fun. For example, Albert Einstein said, "Imagination is more important than intelligence." Watch this:

Dear Audrey,

Imagination is more important than intelligence.

Love, Albert

xoxo

How fun is that? From the beyond, Albert is letting you know some facts about life. This is your world, you can do whatever is going to push you into the next dimension. Some people need a little push, some others need a bulldozer. You know which one you are, and it's not a judgement either. If it takes a bulldozer to get you to run 1,000 miles, then bring on the bulldozer. Who is your bulldozer?

There is someone out there that can really get you into a space of serious action. Is that a friend, is that a sibling, is that a colleague or alum from school? Whoever it is, call on them and let them know what you're up to. Ask them if they want to be your accountability partner. Pick someone good, someone you can count on. Someone that is dependable and just as hungry as you are. No need picking someone you have to spend your time motivating to the gods. Make sure they match your intensity, even a little more. Also, do your part, and make sure it's worth their time also.

Get some rules in place when one of you doesn't meet your goals. What is the language that is appropriate, and what steps must you take to rectify that lapse in forward motion. How will you get each other back on track. This is not a blame game or beat 'em up Scotty, it's a coach that helps you get back in the game. A cheerleader with good intentions. Match their efforts. If they are pushing on the gas, turn it up on your side if you can. Celebrate their wins, and bask in your wins as well.

It may be beneficial to actually have a Life Coach, if you can afford it. There are Life Coaches for personal life, business, spiritual development, and individual goals. Make sure you pick the right one. One that has the expertise you need to guide you in the specific direction you want to go in. Have an introductory session, complimentary if possible, to see if you even vibe with their style. Some coaches have an aggressive approach, and others are more nurturing and feel good types. See what works best for you, but don't shy away from the aggressive types because they can push you in a way that the feel good types won't. It's about results, not fluffy feelings in the end.

You might need to take a class or two. Check out the local college for some certificate programs that can get you up to speed on what you need. You want to be the best you can be no matter what you're doing. There may need to be some refining of your skills. Even if you think you know a lot, going back and reviewing what you think you know can be reassuring, and can build confidence.

Put yourself out there in ways that you would never normally do. If you want to be a stand-up comedian, go to a club and try your hand at an open mic. If you bomb out, perfect, now you know what doesn't work. Sit in the crowd when others are wowing the crowd. In the movie, The Joker, the character sat in the audience with a notepad. You can do that for any area of life, take notes. Somebody already perfected it, so why reinvent the wheel. Put your own spin on it, and make it unique to you.

If you want to be a poet, write some poems, publish them and ask people to read them. Ask for brutal, honest feedback. That can only help you. People are afraid of not being celebrated right out of the gate. Nobody ever masters anything without failing a ton first. I'm sure there are people who believe people come out of the womb as virtuosos, playing Chopin and Bach in the crib, but the truth is, you don't see the hours that person practiced in the dark. There is a lot of sacrifice that comes with mastery. Don't look at the finished product, without going behind the curtain to see the blood, sweat, and tears that produced the shiny emblem on stage. Every diamond traveled a long long way from the caves to get to someone's hand. It took a lot of pressure, heat, travel, and cutting to get to that point. The price represents all of that, not just its place in the window.

Think about what your Execution Plan is going to be. How will you get started? Writing things down is one thing, but putting one foot out in front of the other is something else entirely. How will you maintain the sustained lift?

_____

_____

_____

_____

_____

EXECUTION PLAN:

Step 1: When will you start? _____

Step 2: When will you promote? _____

Step 3: When will you join groups? _____

Step 4: Who's your accountability partner? _____

_____

Step 5: When will you secure that? _____

Step 6: What research do you need to do? _____

_____

Step 7: When will the first fruits appear? _____

Step 8: When will the goal be completed? _____

_____

Step 9: How will you celebrate? _____

_____

Step 10: What's next after this? _____

_____

You have found all of the feathers in your wings!

Chapter 11

Celebration

"The more you praise and celebrate your life,

the more there is in life to celebrate."

Oprah Winfrey

What's the next move, now that you have found your wings? Where will you go? Who will you see? Who will you inspire? Are there people around you that have lost their wings that you can help find them?

It's all about paying it forward. Find some people that you think have lost their wings. Write them here and their email or phone number:

_____

_____

_____

_____

_____

Make a point to contact these people and tell them about your experience with finding your wings. Invite them to a coffee or tea brunch. Buy them a copy of this book. Tell them that you are making an investment into their future.

If you have the time, and you should make the time, make them your own personal cheering section. You will be a part of their cheering section too. Get together on a regular basis, possibly weekends, holidays, breaks, or even on a school night. Anything is possible, if you are determined.

Create a vision board party, a manifestation workshop, or a book club to review the progress with their book. Take no credit for what they accomplish, but make sure you are a leader, meaning you are showing them how to use their wings effectively. Be a beacon of light for everyone that you help to find their wings. Be bold about your successes. Bring them along when you celebrate a new victory, and celebrate them as well. Keep in touch with them on a mailing list, or a group on social media. Keep it active.

These are the ways you celebrate your own awakening. It's not just for you, it's for others to be inspired by it, and to follow your lead. You can send that positivity all across the planet, sometimes by inspiring just one person. I can think of all the people in my lifetime that blessed me with a story of their own triumph. I still think about them today. The conversations are still fresh in my mind, in my back pocket, to pull out whenever I need inspiration. We need each other, and some of us need a little push to motivate us. You may very well be that push for someone. Don't forget to congratulate yourself, and do it often. Spoil Yourself!

Here are ways you can celebrate finding your wings:

1. Schedule a talk at your local church.

2. Do a workshop at your child's school, PTA etc.

3. Get a book club going with your neighbors.

4. Grab a bite with your close friends.

5. Start a blog, and document your experiences.

6. Do a radio show, for free online.

7. Start a podcast that focuses on motivation.

8. Write a book, poem, short story, essay.

9. Publish an Op-Ed piece in your local paper.

10. Post a picture on social media that represents how you are feeling now. If it won't inspire anyone, don't post it.

11. Print out and post a certificate.

12. Go on vacation, and tell someone new your story.

13. Do something you never thought you could do.

14. Start working on that bucket list, 25 things.

15. Do Career Day at a school.

16. Volunteer at a hospital for sick kids.

17. Feed the homeless, bring friends.

18. Volunteer at a homeless shelter for women/kids.

19. Give a single person a Valentine's Gift.

20. Take someone out who has lost a loved one.

21. Call a widow/er on Mother's Day, Father's Day.

22. Do a chore for an elderly senior.

23. Take groceries to a single mother.

24. Visit an orphanage and teach an art class.

25. Create a scavenger hunt for preschoolers.

26. Buy a community center some books.

27. Read to kids at the library.

28. Sing a song at a barber shop.

29. Take a cooking class.

30. Buy a spa day for you and a friend, sibling.

You don't need permission to celebrate. It's your absolute right to celebrate your wins. It's also your absolute right to keep on winning. You don't owe anybody, not even someone connected to you that might feel jealous or envious, to dim your light. Shine it, until it moves them. If they aren't moved by your brilliance, rethink your associations. The greatest way that a person can go farther than they ever expected, is to surround themselves with people that are either going the same way, or as fast as they are.

It can be lonely at the top, but not for long. You have to change your surroundings. Be bold in meeting new people, especially people that can further your goals. People might see that as being an opportunist, but I call it creating opportunities. You are also an opportunity for someone else. Imagine all the people you could assist with your connections that you aren't even using. I have a wealth of knowledge about many things, but since I'm no longer in those fields, I would have to find people who needed what I know. Find them, and they will be so grateful.

We all like to feel useful, needed, and appreciated. The best advice I can give is, do it for the love of giving. If the appreciation doesn't come, trust me when I tell you, there is a force, larger than this world, that sees everything you do. If you can get a smile from the Universe, that's all the appreciation you will ever need. Find your next useful place, and don't stop until you've given all you can. That's what makes this world such a beautiful place to be. It's what we brought into the world, our gifts, not what we can take. People who spend their whole lives, thinking of themselves, really miss the huge blessing of sharing your gifts, and being a blessing to others. Go now, and fly like the WIND! Gooo!

Audrey Mac, is a writer who grew up in the beautiful city of Miami, Florida. From a young age, she enjoyed the power of the pen, as it expresses one's innermost thoughts. She has a passion for helping people achieve their greatest goals through inspiration and motivation. She is a Human Resources professional, with a writing bug. She lives in sunny South Florida, with her family and her Shiba Inu.

Inga Ambrosia is an educator in South Florida. She has a degree in Psychology from Florida International University. As a Life Coach, and a technology business owner, she encourages her clients and students to pursue higher education. Writing is her first love, and she believes that self-discovery is the compass that propels humanity into their own destiny. Inga has been a vegan for 16 years. She lives in South Florida.

Printed in the United States
By Bookmasters